OXFORD
UNIVERSITY PRESS

Great Clarendon Street, Oxford OX2 6DP

Oxford University Press is a department of the University of Oxford. It furthers the University's objective of excellence in research, scholarship, and education by publishing worldwide in

Oxford New York

Auckland Cape Town Dar es Salaam Hong Kong Karachi Kuala Lumpur Madrid Melbourne Mexico City Nairobi New Delhi Shanghai Taipei Toronto

With offices in

Argentina Austria Brazil Chile Czech Republic France Greece Guatemala Hungary Italy Japan Poland Portugal Singapore South Korea Switzerland Thailand Turkey Ukraine Vietnam

OXFORD and OXFORD ENGLISH are registered trade marks of Oxford University Press in the UK and in certain other countries

© Oxford University Press 2008

The moral rights of the author have been asserted

Database right Oxford University Press (maker)

First published 2008

2012 2011 2010 2009 2008
10 9 8 7 6 5 4 3 2 1

All rights reserved. No part of this publication may be reproduced, stored in a retrieval system, or transmitted, in any form or by any means, without the prior permission in writing of Oxford University Press (with the sole exception of photocopying carried out under the conditions stated in the paragraph headed 'Photocopying'), or as expressly permitted by law, or under terms agreed with the appropriate reprographics rights organization. Enquiries concerning reproduction outside the scope of the above should be sent to the ELT Rights Department, Oxford University Press, at the address above

You must not circulate this book in any other binding or cover and you must impose this same condition on any acquirer

Photocopying

The Publisher grants permission for the photocopying of those pages marked 'photocopiable' according to the following conditions. Individual purchasers may make copies for their own use or for use by classes that they teach. School purchasers may make copies for use by staff and students, but this permission does not extend to additional schools or branches

Under no circumstances may any part of this book be photocopied for resale

Any websites referred to in this publication are in the public domain and their addresses are provided by Oxford University Press for information only. Oxford University Press disclaims any responsibility for the content

ISBN: 978 0 19 480059 4

Printed in China

PET Result
FCE Result
CAE Result

Using a dictionary for exams

Peter May

Introduction	2
Using a learner's dictionary ...	
... for tests of reading	4
... for tests of writing	10
... for tests of vocabulary and grammar	16
... for tests of listening	22
... for tests of speaking	24
Table of exam task types and worksheets	26
Explanatory key	28

OXFORD
UNIVERSITY PRESS

Introduction

The learner's dictionary

A monolingual (English–English) learner's dictionary can play an important part in language learning, both inside and outside the classroom. It can also help bring success in exams. Learners' dictionaries are designed to instruct in practical and useful ways, with the needs of the learner given priority. Compare the following extracts from a native-speaker speaker dictionary (first entry) and a learner's dictionary (second entry).

> **glittering** ▶ adjective shining with a shimmering or sparkling light: *glittering chandeliers.*
> ■ impressively successful or elaborate: *a glittering military career.*
> – DERIVATIVES **glitteringly** adverb.

Oxford Dictionary of English

> **glit·ter·ing** /'glɪtərɪŋ/ *adj.* [usually before noun] **1** very impressive and successful: *He has a glittering career ahead of him.* **2** very impressive and involving rich and successful people: *a **glittering** occasion/ceremony* ◇ *a glittering array of stars* **3** shining brightly with many small flashes of light **SYN** SPARKLING: *glittering jewels*

Oxford Advanced Learner's Dictionary, 7th edition

The entry in the learner's dictionary uses simpler language to explain the meaning and show the word in context. It gives useful information on pronunciation and grammar, frequent collocations, and a synonym to help build vocabulary. Some entries also include illustrations.

Learners' dictionaries are available for students at three levels:

- elementary/pre-intermediate
- intermediate
- advanced

The words they contain and the information given about these words are graded accordingly, as can be seen in the following three entries for the word *relax*.

> **relax** 0ᵣ /rɪ'læks/ *verb* (relaxes, relaxing, relaxed /rɪ'lækst/)
> **1** to rest and be calm; to become less worried or angry: *After a hard day at work I spent the evening relaxing in front of the television.*
> **2** to become less tight or to make something become less tight: *Let your body relax.*

Oxford Essential Dictionary

> **relax** /rɪ'læks/ *verb* **1** [I] to rest while you are doing sth enjoyable, especially after work or effort: *This holiday will give you a chance to relax.* ◆ *They spent the evening relaxing in front of the TV.* **SYN** unwind **2** [I] to become calmer and less worried: *Relax – everything's going to be OK!*
>
> **MORE** In informal English **chill out** and **take it easy** can be used instead of **relax**.
>
> **3** [I,T] to become or make sb/sth become less hard or tight: *A hot bath will relax you after a hard day's work.* ◆ *Don't relax your grip on the rope!* **4** [T] to make rules or laws less strict: *The regulations on importing animals have been relaxed.*

Oxford Wordpower Dictionary

> **relax** 0ᵣ /rɪ'læks/ *verb*
> **1** [V] ~ **(with sth)** to rest while you are doing sth enjoyable, especially after work or effort **SYN** UNWIND: *When I get home from work I like to relax with the newspaper.* ◇ *Just relax and enjoy the movie.* ◇ *I'm going to spend the weekend just relaxing.* **2** to become or make sb become calmer and less worried: [V] *I'll only relax when I know you're safe.* ◇ *Relax! Everything will be OK.* [also VN] **3** to become or make sth become less tight or stiff: [V] *Allow your muscles to relax completely.* ◇ [VN] *The massage relaxed my tense back muscles.* ◇ *He **relaxed his grip** on her arm.* ◇ *(figurative) The dictator refuses to relax his grip on power.* **4** [VN] to allow rules, laws, etc. to become less strict: *The council has relaxed the ban on dogs in city parks.* **5** [VN] to allow your attention or effort to become weaker: *You cannot afford to relax your concentration for a moment.*

Oxford Advanced Learner's Dictionary, 7th edition

The entry at the lowest level is clearly shorter, with only the most basic uses of the word given, but it provides essential information on pronunciation and grammar, with examples of how the word is used in practice. The entry in the intermediate dictionary extends the number of uses and examples, with notes in brackets on transitivity. It also gives a synonym, and there is a note on less formal words with the same meaning. At the advanced level, the entry gives a wider range of examples in different contexts, as well as further uses, including a figurative meaning.

A good learner's dictionary contains a huge range of resources for the student. There are extensive reference and practice sections at the beginning, in the middle or at the end of the book. These provide an enormous amount of information on lexis (often through the use of colour pictures), vocabulary learning, pronunciation, grammar and writing skills. There are also practice sections such as the *Wordpower Workout* and the exercises in the Study Pages of the *Oxford Essential Dictionary*, with a key for users. Within the main body of the dictionary, the entries themselves frequently include notes, for instance, on style/register, related words, antonyms, phrasal verbs, or idioms. There may also be boxes next to entries giving useful information on areas such as spelling, vocabulary building, and cultural aspects. Some of these are shown in the examples from the three dictionaries opposite.

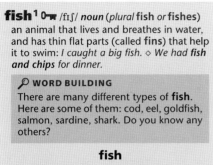

fish¹ 0-ᵣ /fɪʃ/ *noun* (*plural* **fish** *or* **fishes**)
an animal that lives and breathes in water, and has thin flat parts (called **fins**) that help it to swim: *I caught a big fish.* ◇ *We had fish and chips for dinner.*

> 🔎 **WORD BUILDING**
>
> There are many different types of **fish**. Here are some of them: cod, eel, goldfish, salmon, sardine, shark. Do you know any others?

fish

Oxford Essential Dictionary

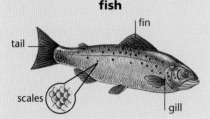

ɪstair /steə(r)/ *noun* **1 stairs** [pl] a series of steps inside a building that lead from one level to another: *a flight of stairs* • *I heard somebody coming down the stairs.* • *She ran up the stairs.* ⊃ picture on **page P4** ⊃ look at **downstairs, upstairs**

> **HELP** Stairs or steps? Stairs or flights of stairs are usually inside buildings. Steps are usually outside buildings and made of stone or concrete.

2 [C] one of the steps in a series inside a building: *She sat down on the bottom stair to read the letter.*

Oxford Wordpower Dictionary

like·ly 0-ᵣ /ˈlaɪkli/ *adj., adv.*
▪ *adj.* (**like·lier, like·li·est**) **HELP** more likely and most likely are the usual forms **1** ~ (**to do sth**) | ~ (**that ...**) probable or expected: *the most likely outcome* ◇ *Tickets are likely to be expensive.* ◇ *It's more than likely that the thieves don't know how much it's worth.* ◇ *They might refuse to let us do it, but it's hardly likely.* **2** seeming suitable for a purpose **SYN** PROMISING: *She seems the most likely candidate for the job.* **IDM** a **'likely story** (*informal, ironic*) used to show that you do not believe what sb has said
▪ *adv.* **IDM** as **,likely as 'not** | **most/very 'likely** very probably: *As likely as not she's forgotten all about it.* **not 'likely!** (*informal, especially BrE*) used to disagree strongly with a statement or suggestion: *Me? Join the army? Not likely!*

> **GRAMMAR POINT**
>
> **likely**
>
> ▪ In standard *BrE* the adverb **likely** must be used with a word such as **most, more** or **very**: *We will most likely see him later.* In informal *NAmE* **likely** is often used on its own: *We will likely see him later.* ◇*He said that he would likely run for President.*

Oxford Advanced Learner's Dictionary, 7th edition

Notice particularly the information on North American usage: while acceptable in an examination such as the FCE or CAE, it must be used consistently.

There are further extensive resources on the *Oxford Essential Dictionary CD-ROM*, the *Oxford Wordpower Dictionary CD-ROM*, and the *Oxford Advanced*

Learner's Compass. Learners can listen to and practise pronunciation, and do vocabulary-related exercises.

A learner's dictionary and exams

A learner's dictionary can be used in these ways:

- Preparation: building vocabulary, spelling and pronunciation, differences in meaning, awareness of appropriacy, improved knowledge of grammar.
- Practice: vocabulary and grammar exercises, and annotated model texts to develop writing skills.
- Self-correction: particularly in Writing and Use of English. Students can correct all their answers, or the teacher can mark them correct or incorrect for students to correct.

Using this booklet

This booklet focuses on ways of using the *Oxford Essential Dictionary*, the *Oxford Wordpower Dictionary*, and the *Oxford Advanced Learner's Dictionary* to develop students' language skills and improve their performance in PET, FCE, and CAE. The five main sections, correspond to the Reading, Writing, Speaking and Listening papers of the exams; the Vocabulary and Grammar section covers PET Reading Part 5 & Writing Part 1, and FCE and CAE Use of English.

Each double-page spread focuses on two exam task-types at the same level, with the recommended dictionary shown at the top of the photocopiable exam worksheet. The teacher's notes on the left explain how the dictionary can be used to prepare for and/or practise the exam tasks on the worksheet. As many task types are used in more than one of the three exams, a note at the top of this page may indicate which others it is relevant to.

The notes for each task-type begin by stating what it tests and how, followed by an outline of what learners need to know and do. The relevance of the dictionary is then explained, and an activity takes learners through the process of finding and using the information contained in the appropriate entry, notes, or study pages. Further practice activities are sometimes suggested. The focus then shifts to the task (usually, for reasons of space, shorter than in the actual exam) on the facing page, where students are shown how they can apply what they have been practising to the exam task. This often involves working through an example item. The students then do the rest of the exam task – with or without their dictionaries – at the teacher's discretion. Finally, they check their answers with the Explanatory Key (at the back of the book). This explains why the correct answers are right and the wrong ones are not. On pages 26–27 there is a table showing the main task types used in the three exams, plus the worksheets that are either specifically designed for them, or relevant to them.

Using a learner's dictionary
for tests of reading

The Reading papers of CAE, FCE, and PET test a range of skills, from text and paragraph level right down to individual words and their synonyms or antonyms. Good dictionaries can help learners prepare for these tasks, either through the comprehensive information within the entries, the extra notes in special boxes next to the entries, or in the many sections of study pages, exercises, and other reference material they contain.

Worksheet 1
Using the Oxford Essential Dictionary

True/False
- PET Reading, Part 3

In Part 3 of PET Reading, students have to scan a text for evidence that each of a series of statements about the text is either true or false. The statements generally use different words from those in the text to say the same, or the opposite, so students need to be able to recognize paraphrase.

The *Oxford Essential Dictionary* can help learners prepare for this task type through the frequent 'same meaning' or 'opposite' notes in entries for common words. Students should be encouraged to write these down in their vocabulary notebooks whenever they look up new words that have these synonyms or antonyms marked.

Preparation Tell the class to look up **clever** in their dictionaries, and find a word with the same meaning (**intelligent**) and one that means the opposite (**stupid**). Get them to look up more words of different kinds, finding antonyms and/or synonyms, e.g. **arrive**, **quiet**, **happily**. Point out that different meanings of the same word may have different synonyms or opposites, e.g. **right** ('wrong' or 'left'), **hard** ('easy' or 'soft'), **light** ('dark' or 'heavy').

1 The class study the instructions for the true/false task opposite, and then the list of statements. Point out that these follow the order of the information in the text, so once they have found the part relevant to one answer they should continue scanning the text until they find the next one. They need to look carefully at each of these, using any synonyms or antonyms (especially in the case of 'false' answers) to help them decide whether the text actually says the same as the statement or not.

2 When they have their four answers, they check them with the explanatory key.

3 Point out that recognition of antonyms, synonyms, and synonymous phrases is tested in other reading and listening task types.

Multiple-choice
- PET Reading, Part 1

In Part 1 of PET Reading, candidates match the meanings of five short texts with the correct option in multiple-choice questions. Possible texts include signs, notices, personal messages, instructions, and labels. To do this task, students need to be able to understand the overall meaning of the texts, which may use few words with little or no context.

Preparation If the class have little experience of this task type, a useful starting point is the *Exam Practice* Part 1 on study page S4 in the *Oxford Essential Dictionary*. Explain that this is a simplified form of the PET task (simpler texts; matching meanings with texts rather than choosing from three options for each) and get them to write down their answers. They then check with the key on page 486.

A difficulty they might have with PET texts is identifying the meaning of key words. For example, 'closed' in a sign such as 'Restaurant closed all day Sunday' (adjective, or past form of verb?); 'lock' as in 'Lock door behind you after entering' (noun, or imperative form of verb?); or the modal 'should' in 'All used bottles should be placed in a separate container' (advice or prediction?). When the class start practising with texts of this kind, let them check in their dictionary whether key words can be other parts of speech, or have other meanings. The word **lock** for instance, has separate entries when used as a *verb* or a *noun*, and **should** has four different meanings, including: 'to tell or ask somebody what is the right thing to do' (advice), and 'to say what you think will happen' (prediction).

1 Focus attention on the multiple-choice task opposite, beginning with the instructions and then the texts. Tell the class to look at each one, deciding where they would see it, who might have written it and for whom. Suggest they form their own idea of what it says before they look at the three options. Advise against choosing one of these options just because it contains a word or words used in the text.

2 They do the task, making sure they know how the key words are used.

3 Finally, they check their answers with the explanatory key.

Worksheet 1

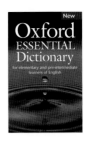

True/False

- Look at the statements below about visiting Sydney.
- Read the extract below to decide if each statement is correct or incorrect.
- If it is correct, mark A.
- If it is not correct, mark B.

1 There are some lovely beaches near Sydney. ......
2 You can cross the bridge on foot without paying. ......
3 A ferry to Manly is more expensive than a water taxi. ......
4 The best time to see Sydney from the ferry is at dawn. ......

A visit to Sydney

There are so many things to do in Sydney that it is difficult to know where to begin. Australia's greatest city (though not its capital) has it all. There's great shopping, exciting nightlife, fantastic views and, not far from the city, beautiful beaches.

Most people start at the South Shore, linked to the northern half of the city by the world-famous Harbour Bridge. You can walk or cycle over free, or, if you can pay $100 and are not scared of heights, climb over! Groups of up to ten people leave every 15 minutes, climbing to the top of the bridge and back down again in two hours.

Probably the best way to see the bridge, though, is from the water below. You can take a tourist boat around the harbour for about $20, or a water taxi for $50, but it's actually cheaper to buy a ticket for a ferry to one of the seaside towns out towards the Pacific. The views of the bridge, the city skyscrapers and the Opera House are just as good, for instance, from the ferry to Manly, which takes just half an hour.

There you will find a good swimming, an excellent funfair and also 'Oceanworld', where those brave enough can swim with sharks. On your return, try to take a ferry that sails back at sunset, which is when Sydney looks more wonderful than ever!

Multiple choice (notices, messages, etc.)

- Look at the text in each question.
- What does it say?
- Mark the correct letter next A, B or C.

> **MOBILE PHONES MAY NOT BE USED IN THIS BUILDING**

1 A Mobiles do not work properly here.
  B You must not use your mobile here.
  C People rarely use their mobiles here.

> Simon – I'm at the café but it's closed until the afternoon. Shall we meet at the bus stop instead? – Martin.

2 A Martin suggests meeting at a different place.
  B Martin wants to know if Simon is at the bus stop.
  C Martin doesn't want to meet Simon today.

> **Nearly-new MP3 player for sale**
>
> Hardly used, but just £30 or best offer.
> Contact Elena Jones, Class 4C

3 A She wants to buy a cheap MP3 player.
  B She might sell the MP3 player for less than £30.
  C She is selling the MP3 player because it is in bad condition.

Worksheet 2
Using the Oxford Wordpower Dictionary

Gapped text (missing sentences)
- FCE Reading, Part 2

In FCE Gapped text, students have to replace seven missing sentences in a long text.

This task type tests awareness of how a text is linked together, in terms of both logical development and language cohesion. The latter involves understanding the use of devices such as reference words (e.g. *that, they, ones*), time markers and lexical sets (e.g. *train, ticket, platform, catch, depart*).

Preparation   One way students can prepare for this task is to learn the words most commonly associated with everyday topics. The *Oxford Wordpower Dictionary* has Topic boxes that cover many of these in a brief context. Begin by telling the class to work through the Topic Notes exercise on page xviii, and checking their answers in the Workout key on page xxiii.

Then refer them to the box just below the entry for **mobile phones**. Point out that the expressions there may be useful to them both when they are speaking and when they are doing reading (or listening) tasks. Explain that, for example, the main text might contain a phrase like *the signal on her mobile was quite weak* and the missing sentence may say *in the end she got through*. Here, the lexical set is *signal/ mobile/got through*. Ask the class to think of more examples like this, using words and phrases from this box, or others such as **shopping**, **sport**, **pets**, **schools**, and **films**.

1   Tell the class to look at the gapped text exercise opposite. Ask them to read the three paragraphs very quickly, ignoring the missing sentences for the moment, and identify the main idea in each (1 the danger of someone else using your Internet connection, 2 how to prevent this 3 the danger from material downloaded from the Internet).

2   They study sentences A–C. Ask which words they think may form a lexical set with others in the main text (e.g. 'virus', 'modem', 'logged on'), and to think about other clues there (e.g. reference words, verb tenses).

3   They do the exam task.

4   They check their answers with the explanatory key when they have finished.

Multiple matching
- FCE Reading, Part 3
- CAE Reading, Part 4
- PET Reading, Part 2

FCE Reading Part 3 tests reading for specific information, by requiring candidates to match prompts with the correct sections of an informative or descriptive text. Although initial gist reading is advisable, the main strategy needed is to scan through the text for words which express the same idea as each prompt. Students may need, therefore, to recognize a number of different expressions commonly used for everyday actions.

Preparation   Students can use the *Oxford Wordpower Dictionary* to help them prepare for this. Refer them to 'Other words for notes' on page xvii of Wordpower Workout and get them to work through exercises A and B, then check their answers with the key on page xxii. Point out that 'other words' does not necessarily mean words of the same class, or even in the same structure, for example: *I think/in my opinion/as far as I'm concerned/it seems to me that*.

Then focus on an actual 'Other words for' box next to an entry, for instance **price**, highlighting the different ways 'charge' and 'cost' are used, and eliciting examples of both as verbs. Point out that forms such as *the price is X* (where X is the amount of money)/*they charge X/it costs X* are typical of the kind of expressions that can indicate a match between prompt and text. Other boxes you might want the class to look at, in addition to those for the words in Wordpower Workout, include allow, **small**, **travel**, **temperature**, and **under**.

1   Tell the class to read very quickly through the four sections of the text opposite to form a general impression.

2   Make sure they understand all the prompts. Tell them to match each of these with the appropriate section by looking very quickly through the text for words or phrases that express the same idea.

3   When they have completed the matching task, they check their answers with the explanatory key.

For CAE Reading, Part 4, see the Synonyms and Which Word? boxes in the *Oxford Advanced Learner's Dictionary*.
For PET Reading, Part 2, see the Which Word? boxes in the *Oxford Essential Dictionary*.

Worksheet 2

Gapped text (sentences)

You are going to read an extract from a magazine article about Internet dangers. Three sentences have been removed from the extract. Choose from the sentences A–C the one which fits each gap (1–3).

It is also possible for somebody else, possibly in a nearby house or car, to access your connection with the Internet without your knowledge or permission. (1) ...... Cases have been reported of criminals using other people's networks in this way to download illegal material, or even to obtain private information about bank accounts.

Fortunately, there is an easy way to avoid this happening. On your computer, you simply select 'secured' for your wireless link, and choose a password. Then, the next time you want to go the Internet, you key in your password at the prompt. (2) ...... Anyone trying to use your network will be unable to do so without the password.

However, this does nothing to protect you from the many dangers that lie online. You need to be particularly careful when downloading material such as music files, or when receiving emails with documents attached to them. (3) ...... It is advisable not to open these at all.

A These, especially if you don't know the sender, might contain a virus.

B This may be a real risk if you use a wireless modem.

C When you have logged on, your connection is now completely secure.

Multiple matching

You are going to read an advertisement for property for rent. For questions 1–4, choose from the sections (A–D). The sections may be chosen more than once.

Which property would suit somebody who ...

would like to live alone?	1 ...
doesn't enjoy cleaning?	2 ...
wants to live in a quiet area?	3 ...
likes outdoor activities?	4 ...

PROPERTY TO LET

A This modern house on the outskirts of town has two bedrooms, a living room, a dining room, kitchen and bathroom – all beautifully furnished. There is also a large garden, which backs onto open countryside. Perfect if you are keen on walking or cycling.

B This is a bright and sunny studio apartment, with great views across the city centre. It is also extremely compact, making the most of the available space. If you prefer somewhere on your own, this is the ideal place for you.

C This bungalow has three large bedrooms, a lounge and dining area, two bathrooms and a spacious kitchen. It also has a double garage. Although it does not have a garden, the property is located in an exclusive district, well away from the noise of the city centre.

D This luxurious one-bedroom flat consists of a lounge, dining-room, fitted kitchen and bathroom. The building has its own private garden and 24-hour security. Services provided include laundry and cleaning, so you won't need to do any housework at all!

Worksheet 3
Using the Oxford Advanced Learner's Dictionary

Gapped text (missing paragraphs)
- CAE Reading, Part 2

Part 2 of CAE Reading tests overall comprehension and text structure by requiring candidates to replace missing paragraphs. To do this, students need to understand how the text is organized and how it fits together in terms of coherence and cohesion.

Although, in practical terms, this task type is mainly about putting the right main point in the right place, language clues are also important. These include reference words like *this, it* and *them*; lexical links such as synonyms, antonyms and repetition of the same word; and linking expressions, particularly conjunctions of time, cause/result and contrast.

Students at this level should be familiar with many of the more basic expressions, e.g. *after that, as a result of, in spite of*, but they may be unsure of others. Some might be confusing (*eventually* is a false cognate in certain languages) and others use common words with different meanings, sometimes in idiomatic phrases. Examples include *still* and *then again*.

Preparation Focus attention on 'yet' or 'and yet' as linkers, possibly by writing an example on the board, e.g. *The ground was wet. Yet there had been no rain last night.* Then tell the class to use the *Oxford Advanced Learner's Dictionary* to find out the meaning in this case, which probably differs from those they are familiar with (when used as an adverb). The answer is in the part of the entry marked 'conj', which gives the meaning, the synonym 'nevertheless', and two example sentences.

Point out that 'yet' is used here for concession, a contrast in which something unexpected is stated or implied. Give more examples: *even though people are living longer, the population is declining* and elicit other expressions used in this way (*even so, much as, no matter what*, etc.), getting the class to look them up for the precise meaning and further examples.

1 Tell the class to study the exam task opposite, bearing in mind this is an extract, not a complete text. Point out that all five paragraphs contain a linking expression in the first sentence, although one of these (the time link 'since then') would refer back to a previous part of the text that is not shown. You may also want to explain that they are five different types of link (time, reason, concession, contrast, and reference).

2 Tell them first to read the five paragraphs for a general idea of this part of the text, and for the main idea of each paragraph.

3 They try to fit the missing paragraphs into the correct spaces based on this, and use the linkers as clues.

4 They check their answers with the explanatory key.

This approach is also relevant to FCE Reading, Part 2 (missing sentences). See the entries for linking expressions in the *Oxford Wordpower Dictionary*.

Multiple-choice questions
- CAE Reading, Part 1 and Part 3
- FCE Reading, Part 1

Part 1 of CAE Reading uses two multiple-choice questions for each of three short texts, while Part 3 has a longer text and seven of these questions. These may test comprehension of a number of features, including the writer's attitude and opinions. Appreciating the tone used may be important here, but candidates might also need to understand the words used – particularly in the four options – to describe what the writer thinks or feels.

Preparation Students can help prepare for this kind of question by developing their awareness of tone in writing, and by broadening their knowledge of the adjectives and nouns used to describe attitude and opinion, e.g. *disappointed/disappointment, bored/boredom*, together with their synonyms and antonyms. Tell the class to look up **astonished** in the *Oxford Advanced Learner's Dictionary* and elicit the meaning ('very surprised'), a synonym marked SYN ('amazed') and, in a lower entry, the noun ('astonishment'). Then do the same with **optimistic**, eliciting the synonym given ('positive'), the antonym marked OPP ('pessimistic'), and the noun higher up ('optimism'). Get the class, possibly in groups, to brainstorm more of these, look them up in the same way and write them down in their vocabulary notebooks.

1 Focus attention on the text and two questions opposite. Tell them to highlight the key adjectives in both sets of options A–D (1 convinced, sceptical, open-minded, dismissive; 2 indifferent, critical, sympathetic, amused). You may want to let them look up some or all of these words at this stage, especially any that may be false cognates in the students' first language.

2 If they have not already done so, they use their dictionaries to check their answers when they have finished.

3 They confirm or check their answers by referring to the explanatory key.

This activity is also relevant to CAE and FCE Listening multiple-choice questions.

For FCE Reading, Part 1, see the *Oxford Wordpower Dictionary*.

Worksheet 3

Gapped text (paragraphs)

You are going to read an extract from an article. Three paragraphs have been removed from the extract. Choose from the paragraphs A–C the one which fits each gap (1–3).

---

1 ....

Programmes **of this nature** (*reference*) have used unreliable data and unscientific projections. A wholly improbable scenario has been created, in which old age pensioners form the majority and children no longer exist, of a welfare system permanently in crisis because there is virtually nobody of working age left.

2 ....

Conversely (*contrast*), the figure for those aged 65 and over is forecast to rise from under 10 million at present to about 15 million over the same period. In fact, the number of people of 60 and over already exceeds the number of children in the UK.

3 ....

A **All the same** (*concession*), there can be little doubt that overall the age profile of the population is likely to change significantly over the coming decades, with appreciable consequences for society and the economy. A recent report, based on rigorous research, indicates that the number of people under the age of 15 will decline from around 11 million in 2000 to below 9 million by 2040.

B **Since then** (*time*), there have been several television documentaries on the theme of the increasing number of older people in society. Unfortunately, all of them have exaggerated the rate of change in the age structure of the population, and used this to make unfounded predictions of widespread economic and social collapse.

C **On account of this** (*reason*), there will indeed be a reduction in the working population of this country. However, this is forecast to fall from the current figure of approximately 47.5% of the total population, to 44.5% by 2030 – hardly the catastrophic shift predicted on TV.

Multiple-choice questions

For questions 1 and 2, choose the answer (A, B, C, or D) which you think fits best according to the text.

A current study of over 1000 office staff seems to show that ever-increasing numbers of emails are having a serious effect on productivity, by making office workers unable to concentrate on a given task for any length of time. The problem, apparently, is that staff react in a totally undisciplined way when emails arrive, dropping whatever they are doing to read and reply to the latest message, whatever the topic. This constant changing of focus, the researchers say, leads to mental fatigue and even a lowering of intelligence. The study is not yet complete, but they may have a point and it will be interesting to see their findings when they are published.

It might also be instructive to study the effects on performance of the growing tendency for meetings to come to a stop every time someone receives an email.

This, they believe, whatever the subject, has to be answered immediately, so the individual concerned mumbles an apology or gives a weak smile and then proceeds to hold up everything while they key in their reply. They may feel it's a sign of efficiency, but the reality is that it's frustrating for everyone else – and extremely bad manners.

---

1 What does the writer feel about the volume of emails that staff receive?
  A She is convinced that it damages efficiency.
  B She is sceptical about whether it does any harm to efficiency.
  C She is open-minded about the idea that it harms efficiency.
  D She is dismissive of the suggestion that it damages efficiency.

2 When people break off meetings to answer emails, the writer is …
  A indifferent to the interruptions.
  B critical of their rude behaviour.
  C sympathetic towards them.
  D amused by the situation.

Using a learner's dictionary
for tests of writing

The Writing papers of CAE, FCE, and PET test many different skills, requiring two pieces of writing (PET Writing, Part 1 is more a test of grammar). In the two higher-level exams there are many possible text types. A good dictionary can help students prepare for all of these. They can use the entries for specific words, boxes with extra information, study pages, exercises, and reference sections, including pages on specific task types such as letter writing. Here, as elsewhere, there is useful information on style and register. Students can also check their work for accurate spelling and use of linking expressions.

Worksheet 4
Using the Oxford Essential Dictionary

Writing a story
* PET Writing, Part 3
* FCE Writing, Part 2

Part 3 of PET Writing tests coherent organization, the use and control of a range of language up to CEF level B1, and punctuation. Spelling is also assessed, with marks lost for errors that interfere with communication. Students therefore need to be able to write words accurately, and to check their completed work for spelling mistakes.

It is impossible, however, to look up the spelling of every word either while writing or afterwards as a check. The emphasis needs to be on noting the spelling of each new word as it is learnt, and knowing which words are likely to cause them difficulties. This may depend partly on whether cognates in their own language have slightly different spelling. They also need to know what kind of errors can seriously interfere with communication.

Preparation   Give the class examples of ambiguity caused by misspelling, e.g. *I had a dream about a huge dessert* (desert) or *We crossed the churchyard at an angel* (angle), then point out that the *Oxford Essential Dictionary* has boxes headed SPELLING next to entries for words that frequently cause difficulties. Tell the class to look up **accept** and **excellent**, find a common misspelling of each and decide which might impede communication (EXCEPT), and which probably would not (EXCELLENT). Do the same with more words, such as **disappointed**, **receive**, **diary**, **unnecessary**, and **grammar**.

1   Focus on the example in the exam task opposite, asking whether the mistake would impede understanding at all. They may feel it could, as the reader might have to stop and think whether the writer really means 'forty' – or 'four'.

2   They do the correction task.

3   They check their answers with the explanatory key, and their dictionary.

For FCE Writing, Part 2, see the *Oxford Wordpower Dictionary*, page iv (*irregular spelling*) and S40.

Message
* PET Writing, Part 2

In Part 2 of PET Writing, candidates have to show they can write a short message, following precise instructions and using language accurately. They will need to know quite a wide range of words to be able to do this, so vocabulary building is vital.

Preparation   The *Oxford Wordpower Dictionary* can help in a number of ways. Next to the entries for certain key words, Word Building notes give information on related words, which may include a number of examples, e.g. **jewel** lists *diamond, emerald, pearl* and *ruby*. Some entries are cross-referenced to the highly useful Picture Dictionary in the middle of the book. Look, for instance, at the entry for **car** and then the picture on colour page P1. There are also Culture notes at some entries, e.g. **birthday**. These give background information that may be useful when writing to 'an English friend', as exam rubrics sometimes specify.

Ask the class all the names of sports they can think of, then tell them to check and look for more on pages P14–15 of their dictionary. Do the same with other topics, jobs, shops and clothes. Turn to the word building notes, eliciting specific information from certain entries. For example, ask what type of tickets you can buy on a bus, what happens in a hospital and what kinds of restaurant there are. Other useful notes include those for colour, exam, hair, job, supermarket, money, and wedding. Finally, refer students to an example of a Culture note at foot, pound, or pint and elicit some equivalent measures.

1   They read the instructions and complete the sample message, referring to the entries and notes in their dictionary, and to the Picture Dictionary where this is indicated in the entry.

2   They check their answers with the explanatory key.

3   As a follow-up, they write a message of their own, based on the same instructions.

Worksheet 4

Story

- Your English teacher has asked you to write a story.
- Your story must have the following title:
  A frightening experience
- Write your **story** in about 100 words.

Find and correct eight spelling mistakes in this sample story, as in the example. Which of these could impede understanding?

I was on a school trip with about ~~fourty~~ *forty* other pupils when we walked into the forest. Imediately, it became very dark as the bright sun dissappeared. I was at the back of the group and everyone accept me was walking quickly. Suddenly I realised I was alone. I didn't want to loose my way so I turned back and went in the oposite direction, walking untill I came out of the forest again. There I saw a peice of paper lying on the ground. It was a map, and below the name and adress of my school it said 'Danger – keep out of the forest'.

Message

Read the exam instructions and then complete the message.

You want to cook a meal for an English friend of yours called Sam.

Write an e-mail to send to Sam. In your e-mail, you should

- invite Sam to eat at your house
- say what you will cook
- suggest a time.

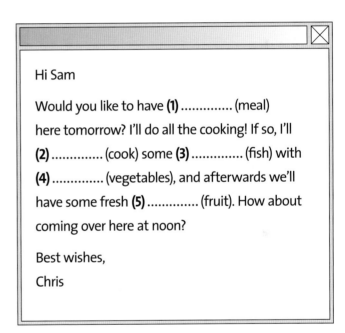

Hi Sam

Would you like to have **(1)** .... (meal) here tomorrow? I'll do all the cooking! If so, I'll **(2)** .... (cook) some **(3)** .... (fish) with **(4)** .... (vegetables), and afterwards we'll have some fresh **(5)** .... (fruit). How about coming over here at noon?

Best wishes,

Chris

Worksheet 5
Using the Oxford Wordpower Dictionary
Essay
- FCE Writing, Part 2
- CAE Writing, Part 2

Writing an essay, or composition, is one of the possible task types in FCE Writing, Part 2. The context given is often that of a teacher setting work following a classroom discussion. An important factor in the successful completion of the task is cohesion, particularly the use of suitable linking words and phrases. In addition to the information on linkers in specific entries, the *Oxford Wordpower Dictionary* has a section entitled Essay Writing on study page S44 which contains categories of linkers, examples of them in context, and other useful information and advice.

Preparation Ask the class which linking expressions, e.g. *secondly*, *to sum up*, they know and get them to look some of them up in their dictionary. Point out that the entries will give their meaning, plus an example of the expression in use. Then refer them to study page S44 of the *Oxford Wordpower Dictionary* telling them to read 'Before you start', especially the linking expressions in context, and the six categories in 'More linking expressions'.

1 Tell the class to study the list of expressions in the box on the opposite page and put them into the following categories: introduction, more information, consequences, giving examples, opinions, contrast, conclusion.

2 Then look at the exam task, focusing first on the question and then on the sample essay. Ask the class how the essay is organized (1 introduction 2 arguments for the statement   3 arguments against the statement   4 conclusion) and whether they think this text is a good answer for FCE level (yes).

3 Finally, get them to fill in the gaps using the words given. You may want to point out that *furthermore* and *moreover* are interchangeable; the others are not. When they have finished, they check their answers with the explanatory key.

4 As a follow-up, ask them to think of other words and phrases that could go into each gap, e.g. 1 *today, these days, currently, at present, at the moment.*

For further practice with linking expressions in essays, see pages 22–23 of the *Oxford Wordpower Trainer*.
For CAE Writing, Part 2, see the *Oxford Advanced Learner's Dictionary*, reference pages R50–51.

Informal letter
- FCE Writing, Part 2
- PET Writing, Part 3
- CAE Writing, Part 2

Another possible Part 2 task (also in Part 1, though with more input material) is 'writing an informal letter'. Candidates must lay out their letters correctly, write in an appropriate style and use suitable expressions, particularly for beginning and ending their text.

Preparation Show the class the Informal Letters section on study page S42 of the *Oxford Wordpower Dictionary*, drawing their attention to the layout (although you may want to point out it is not normally necessary in exams to include addresses). Then explain that letters in English, as in other languages, use certain expressions for different purposes within the letter. Write these on the board (in jumbled order, with a strong class):

> 1 to greet the reader
> 2 to ask about the reader
> 3 to apologize
> 4 to say why you are writing
> 5 to ask for a reply
> 6 to close the letter
> 7 to add extra information

Tell the class to find the key words used in the letter from Vicky for each.

(1 Dear   2 How   3 Sorry   4 I'm writing to 5 hear from you   6 Love   7 P.S.)

1 Focus on the sample letter opposite. Tell the class to use the correct form of the words and phrases they have practised with Vicky's letter (including alternative endings such as *Take care*).

2 When they have finished, they check with the explanatory key.

3 You may want them to write a letter of their own using the same instructions.

See 'formal letter' on the following pages for differences in style.

For PET Writing, Part 3, see the *Oxford Essential Dictionary*, study page S14.
For CAE Writing, Part 2, see the *Oxford Advanced Learner's Dictionary*, reference page R55.

Worksheet 5

Essay

You have had a class discussion on where the food we eat comes from. Your teacher has now asked you to write an essay giving your opinion on the following statement.

'We should only eat food produced in our own country.'

Use each expression in the box once only to complete the sample essay.

furthermore	to conclude	therefore
however	in my opinion	nowadays
on the other hand	firstly	for instance
moreover		

(1) .... , an increasing proportion of what we eat is imported from distant parts of the world, bringing us a wide variety of food all year round. (2) .... , there are strong arguments both for and against this.

(3) .... , shipping or flying huge quantities of these products inevitably leads to greater air pollution, which is changing the world's climate. (4) .... , all these imports are ruining our own farmers, who cannot compete with lower costs abroad.

(5) .... , as our climate is not as warm as that of countries producing citrus fruits, (6) .... , heating would be required to grow them here. (7) .... , any reduction in pollution caused by transport would be lost because of increased energy use. (8) .... , the consequences for farming families in the exporting countries would be disastrous.

(9) .... , it would not reduce pollution and could harm some of the poorest people in the world. (10) .... , it would be a mistake to eat only home-grown produce.

Informal letter

Read the exam instructions and then complete the sample letter.

Write your answer in **120–180** words in an appropriate style.

Some weeks ago, you went to live in another town. You have now decided to write a letter to a friend in your old town.

Write your **letter**, describing your impressions of the new town and the people there.

(1) .... Jan,

(2) .... 's everything going there? I hope you and your family are all keeping well. I'm (3) .... not to have written sooner, but, as I'm sure you can imagine, I've been terribly busy during these first few weeks. I've had to get used to the new school, and I'm still trying to find my way around!

Anyway, (4) .... say that all's well here. At first the place seemed a little strange and of course I didn't know anyone, but I'm settling in now and I've already made a couple of friends. Most people here are really friendly and there are some good places to go, like the theme park on the edge of town. It'd be great to go there together if you could visit me sometime!

Looking forward to (5) .... soon.

(6) .... ,

Mel

(7) .... It's only a month till the summer holidays. Could you come over then?

Worksheet 6

Using the Oxford Advanced Learner's Dictionary

Article

- CAE Writing, Parts 1 and 2
- FCE Writing, Part 2

A possible task in CAE Writing, Part 1 or Part 2 is 'writing an article'. This can be formal or informal in style, depending on the target reader(s), but should always aim to catch the reader's attention and hold it throughout. An important factor in any text, but especially where a key aim is to make it as readable is possible, is correct punctuation.

Preparation   Learners can help prepare for this (and/or check their work) by studying the Punctuation section on reference pages R60–62 of the *Oxford Advanced Learner's Dictionary*. Encourage particular attention to any punctuation marks that are used differently, or not at all, in the students' first language. This could be the case, for instance, for quotation marks (a dash used instead), the question mark (inverted at the beginning of questions in Spanish), or the apostrophe (not used at all). Check the class are familiar with all of them by setting a 'multiple-matching' type of scanning activity:

> *Which punctuation mark is used:*
> 1 *to show that letters have been left out?*
> 2 *to show that words have been left out?*
> 3 *to show that a list follows?*
> 4 *to add a cross-reference?*
> 5 *to show direct speech?*
> 6 *to follow some abbreviations?*
> 7 *to form a compound?*
> 8 *to show surprise?*
> 9 *to separate a non-defining relative clause?*
> 10 *to separate elements in a website address?*

Go through the answers (1 apostrophe   2 dots 3 colon   4 brackets   5 quotation marks   6 full stop 7 hyphen   8 exclamation mark   9 comma   10 slash or full stop) and do further work on any they have found difficult.

1   The class read the instructions in the Worksheet opposite and punctuate the extract from the sample article. Emphasize that there are often different ways of punctuating a given text, particularly in some uses of commas, but that the aim is to make it as easy to read as possible.

2   Tell them to check with the suggested answer in the explanatory key, and discuss any alternatives.

3   Possibly set the exam task for homework.

Formal letter

- CAE Writing, Parts 1 and 2
- FCE Writing, Parts 1 and 2

Candidates may have to write a formal letter in either Part of CAE Writing. This task requires the use of a consistently appropriate style/register, quite different from the more conversational language that may be suitable in an informal letter.

PREPARATION Tell the class to read the *Labels* section inside the front cover of the *Oxford Advanced Learner's Dictionary* and then ask them what style certain words are, e.g. **prohibit** (formal), **hanky** (informal). Remind them to put 'formal', 'informal', 'slang', etc. in their vocabulary notebooks next to the words they learn that fall into these categories.

Go on to reference pages R53–55, which contain three examples of formal letters and a lot of useful information. Letters of application are quite a common task in CAE Writing, so focus attention on *Applying for a job* on reference pages R53–54. Point out that the notes alongside the letter highlight some aspects of formal writing style, then ask the class to decide which of 1–10 are features of formal writing, giving examples from this letter if they are.

1   formal greeting (yes – *Ms* + surname)
2   contracted forms like *don't* (no)
3   formal expressions (yes – *Please find enclosed ...*)
4   simple linkers like *then* (no)
5   slang words (no)
6   formal words (yes – *wish [to]*)
7   exclamation marks (no)
8   longer, more complex sentences (yes – *I would welcome ...*)
9   formal ending (yes – *Yours sincerely*)
10   full name written out (yes – *Mark Wallace*)

Elicit some other features of formal writing, such as passive verb forms and the less frequent use of phrasal verbs or abbreviations.

1   Tell the class to study the extract from a sample letter opposite, and replace the inappropriate words and phrases with more formal expressions.

2   They check their answers with the explanatory key.

3   You may wish to set the exam writing task for homework.

For FCE Writing, see Formal Letters in the *Oxford Wordpower Dictionary*, study pages S41–43.

Worksheet 6

Article

An international magazine for young people has asked readers to contribute articles in English about their favourite sport or hobby. Articles should describe the following:

- why you first took up this activity and how long you have been doing it
- what you particularly like about it and what you want to do in the future
- what difficulties there are and what you can do to overcome them
- what advice you would give to someone thinking of taking it up

Write your article in **220–260** words.

Punctuate this extract from a sample article, using capital letters where necessary.

> It was about three years ago I think when I first saw people breaking a block of wood with their bare hands my first thought was ouch and my second was Ill never be able to do that then I saw a tiny eleven year old casually walk up and do it and I said to myself why not
>
> Since then apart from one month when I was injured Ive been to Taekwondo classes three times a week reaching green belt my aim is to become a black belt in three years time the training is hard but fun and it makes you feel good about yourself stronger fitter and more confident you make new friends too particularly among those youve started out with

Formal letter

You have seen this advertisement in a local English-language newspaper.

> Applications are invited from students to work as travel guides during the summer months. All nationalities are welcome to apply, although the ability to communicate well in English is essential. The work will be demanding, involving long hours and some weekends, and at times will require patience and understanding with groups of children. If you are interested, tell us why you feel you are the right person for the job, and how you would make a visit to this country a wonderful experience.
>
> Write to: Maria Henderson, Global Travel Ltd.

Write your letter of application in **220–260** words.

Study this extract from a sample letter. Find twenty inappropriate uses of language and replace them with more formal words or phrases.

> Dear Maria,
>
> I am writing to apply for the job of summer travel guide, as advertised in 2day's newspaper. From the info in the ad, it looks dead interesting. As you will see from the stuff in my enclosed CV, I have loads of experience working with guys from all over the world.
>
> Although I'm still a student myself, for several years I have worked with kids on summer camps both here and abroad. So, I am used to working hard to ensure that people have a gr8 holiday. And, I reckon I would be ideally suited to this work seeing as how I am so clued-up on this part of the country, having travelled to every bit of it with my dad or my mates.

Using a learner's dictionary
for tests of vocabulary and grammar

All the task types in FCE and CAE Use of English, as well as Reading, Part 5 and Writing, Part 1 (PET), focus either on vocabulary, grammar, or a mixture of both. Students can help prepare for these tasks by using a dictionary to expand their vocabulary and improve their knowledge of grammatical forms. A good dictionary can make working through practice tests or past papers a part of the whole learning process, and not just testing, by helping them choose the right word or use the correct structure. They can also use their dictionary to check their completed work.

Worksheet 7
Using the Oxford Essential Dictionary
Sentence transformations
- PET Writing, Part 1

Sentence transformations test comprehension and use of a range of grammatical forms up to CEF level B1. Students should therefore be encouraged, whenever they look words up, to study the structures they are used in, paying particular attention to example phrases or sentences.

Preparation   Tell the class to look, for instance, at the verb **help** in the *Oxford Essential Dictionary*, and ask what structures are shown for each use. Next, get them to look up **used to**. Focus first on the structures in the entry (*used to* + infinitive + *when* + simple past; *used to* + infinitive + *but now* + simple present), then on the GRAMMAR note. Explain that there are similar notes for many 'difficult' grammar points – which may be tested in PET sentence transformations. Point out that completing these requires identifying the target structures, and that picking out the key words in the sentences they are given may help with this.

1   Look at the example in Worksheet 7 and elicit the key word (**advised**), the testing focus (changing verb form to noun form) and possible difficulties (a spelling change, an uncountable noun, the correct determiner if used).

2   They then look up **advise** and **advice** in the *Oxford Essential Dictionary*, studying the entries and the GRAMMAR notes for both. If 'advice' is countable in their own language, ask whether this could lead to errors in English and elicit other words that could cause similar problems, e.g. *information, equipment, furniture.*

3   Finally, they do the five questions, highlighting the key words and identifying the structures tested.

4   When they have finished, they check their answers with the explanatory key.

Multiple-choice cloze
- PET Reading, Part 5

Multiple-choice cloze tests understanding of vocabulary and grammar in the context of a short reading text. Candidates have to choose one correct word from four, so they need to know the difference between lexis with similar meanings, and also between structures that vary in meaning according to the use of a single word. Dictionary entries giving the precise meaning and usage of such words are helpful, and the *Oxford Essential Dictionary* also has Which Word? notes next to many that are frequently confused.

Preparation   Tell the class to look up the verb **say** and explain how it differs in usage from 'tell'. Then get them to look up **tell** and ask how that entry helps them do the same: 'Look at the note at say'. Remind the class to write their own examples of words in use when they check them in their dictionary.

1   Focus attention on the multiple-choice cloze test opposite, which is approximately half PET length. Point out that the first thing to do is get an overall impression of the text, so allow a minute or two for them to read it without trying to fill in any gaps. Set some simple gist questions to give them a reason for reading, such as 'What social problem is it about?'

2   Work through the example, looking at each option in turn with reference to the dictionary. Ask what part of speech **every** is, and whether, therefore, it is possible here (there is no noun). Get them to check the first use given in the entry for **anyone** and ask whether the clause containing item 0 is interrogative or negative; (it isn't). Then they look at the entry for **everybody**, where a Which Word? note explains the difference from 'somebody', showing why C is correct.

3   Tell the class to do the remaining five questions, looking up all the options as they do so.

4   Finally, they check their answers with the explanatory key.

Worksheet 7

Sentence transformations

Here are some sentences about tourism.

For each question, complete the second sentence so that it means the same as the first.

Use no more than three words.

Example:

0 The travel agent advised us where to stay.

The travel agent gave us .... **on where to stay.**

Answer: | **0** | *some advice* |

1 The hotel room wasn't big enough for two people.

The hotel room was .... small for two people.

2 They don't let you use your camera in the museum.

You are not .... use your camera in the museum.

3 'I can see the Eiffel Tower,' said Maria.

Maria said she .... the Eiffel Tower.

4 In each hotel room there is an Internet connection.

All hotel rooms have .... own Internet connection.

5 The view was so wonderful that I took some photos.

It was .... wonderful view that I took some photos.

Multiple-choice cloze

Read the text below and choose the correct word for each space.

For each question, mark the correct letter **A**, **B**, **C**, or **D**.

Example answer: 0 *C*

> Regular exercise is something that **(0)** .... needs, but it seems that people in **(1)** .... countries are doing less and less of it. Nowadays, most European adults have a **(2)** .... in an office, and every day they do the **(3)** .... there and back by car or bus, rarely on foot. They **(4)** .... most of their shopping on the Internet and spend much of their free time **(5)** .... TV.

0 A every   B anyone   Ⓒ everybody   D somebody

1 A lot   B some   C any   D much

2 A job   B task   C duty   D work

3 A voyage   B travel   C tour   D journey

4 A pay   B spend   C do   D make

5 A seeing   B looking   C watching   D looking at

Worksheet 8
Using the Oxford Wordpower Dictionary

Open cloze
- FCE Use of English, Part 2
- CAE Use of English, Part 2

Open cloze tests both grammar and vocabulary in a short text containing single-word gaps. A wide range of possible items includes verb forms, quantifiers, relatives, modals, pronouns, comparatives, and phrasal verbs. Where a phrasal verb is tested, the word required may be either the verb or the adverb particle, and students need a wide knowledge of two-part or three-part verbs.

Preparation   Explain to the class that a good dictionary clearly indicates phrasal verbs within the entry for individual verbs. Refer them to page iv of the *Oxford Wordpower Dictionary* and how they are marked (PHR V). Then ask what they think 'sth' stands for ('something') and what particle, in this example, is used with the verb ('up'). Remind the class that some verbs, e.g. **get**, have many more associated phrasal verbs, which themselves can have a number of different meanings, e.g. 'get on'. To illustrate and practise this, get them to work through the exercises in 'Finding phrasal verbs – fast!' on page vii of the Wordpower Workout. When they have finished, use the key on page 30 to go through the answers.

1   Tell the class that the cloze extract in the Worksheet opposite focuses entirely on phrasal verbs. Set some simple questions, such as 'Which part of her journey does the paragraph cover?' (from her house to the airport), and get them to gist read the text in a minute or two.

2   Focus on the example (0), pointing out that although more than one word is sometimes possible as the answer, only one word may be given. Ask what is being tested (the particle) and tell them to study the entry for the verb **set** in their dictionary. Ask how many phrasal verbs are given there in total (12) and how many meanings there are for **set out** and **set off** (2 each). Remind them that the grammar and overall meaning of the text determine what is meant here.

3   The class then fill in gaps 1–6, using their dictionaries as they do so. Where the particle, not the verb, is given, they will have to use their knowledge of phrasal verbs and look at the relevant entry for the verb.

4   When they have finished, they check their answers with the explanatory key.

5   Point out that phrasal verbs are tested in other task types, such as multiple-choice cloze and transformations.

For CAE Use of English, Part 2, see the *Oxford Advanced Learner's Dictionary*, reference pages R40–41.

Word formation
- FCE Use of English, Part 3
- CAE Use of English, Part 3

This task type uses a short text to test ability to form words in a variety of ways: making compounds, changing internal spelling and adding affixes, particularly suffixes. Further changes such as adding verb tense or plural endings may also be required. The ideal preparation for word formation, therefore, is the same kind of word-building approach used to build vocabulary, together with an awareness of how grammatical constraints may determine the exact form of the word in context.

Preparation   An excellent starting point is the 'Build your vocabulary' section on page xvi of the *Oxford Wordpower Dictionary*. Study the example (**attract**) in the table, then elicit the noun and adjective forms of 'deepen', pointing out the internal change to 'depth', as well as the other possible forms of the verb (deepened, deepening) and noun (depths). Then tell them to work through exercises A, B and C. Go through the answers given on page xxii, explaining that many of the words in the table are possible target items in FCE Word formation.

Get the class to study the lists on reference pages S21–22 in the same dictionary, then practise scanning through the affixes by asking them to guess the meanings of words such as 'mishear' or 'clarify'. Some of the affixes may be similar in their own language: suggest they memorise those that are not.

1   Introduce the Word formation task in the Worksheet opposite by setting one or more questions on the main points, e.g. 'Which four features of running a business are mentioned?' (the items, the shop, the staff, and the prices).

2   Focus attention on the example (0), asking what part of speech is required here (adjective) and how they know (it follows an article and precedes a noun). Then refer them to the table on Wordpower Workout page xvi and the suffixes on reference page S22, highlighting the note in brackets following '-ful' in the latter: 'to make adjectives'.

3   Tell them to do questions 1–6, in each case deciding what part of speech is needed and using the above dictionary pages to help them choose the correct affix.

4   They check their answers with the explanatory key.

For CAE Use of English, Part 3, see the *Oxford Advanced Learner's Dictionary*, reference pages R72–75.

Worksheet 8

Open cloze

For questions 1–6, read the text below and think of the word which best fits each gap. Use only **one** word in each space. There is an example at the beginning (0).

Example: 0 *out/off*

ON HER WAY TO INDIA

The next day, Emma set **(0)** .... on her long journey, leaving the house at six o'clock on a cold and foggy morning. At 6.45 she got **(1)** .... the airport bus, but after a few miles it gradually slowed **(2)** .... and then stopped. An old car had **(3)** .... down, holding up all the traffic. After about half an hour, the bus slowly started moving again. Eventually it reached the airport and Emma got **(4)** .... at Terminal 3. She walked quickly through the hall to the Air India counter, where she checked **(5)** .... her small suitcase. Her plane to Mumbai was going to **(6)** .... off in less than an hour, so she had to hurry.

Word formation

For questions 1–6, read the text below. Use the word given in capitals at the end of some of the lines to form a word that fits in the gap **in the same line**. There is an example at the beginning (0).

Example: 0 *successful*

RUNNING A CLOTHES SHOP

Running a clothes shop as a **(0)** .... business is never easy.	SUCCESS
There has to be an extremely wide range of **(1)** .... items	FASHION
on sale, all displayed in the most **(2)** .... manner possible. In	ATTRACT
addition, the **(3)** .... of the	APPEAR
shop should make people want to go inside and spend some time (and money) there. The choice of staff is very important. All shop **(4)** .... should be of about the	ASSIST
same age as the likely customers. They should be friendly and **(5)** .... Above all, the prices	HELP
must be fair: in the end it never pays to **(6)** .... customers. If	CHARGE
they feel they've paid too much, they won't shop there again.	

Worksheet 9

Using the Oxford Advanced Learner's Dictionary

Gapped sentences

- CAE Use of English, Part 4

Part 4 of CAE Use of English assesses knowledge of lexical patterns by focusing either on various meanings of a word, or on various contexts in which a word can be used with the same meaning. The word remains the same part of speech in all three sentences. To do this task, students need to know a wide range of these patterns and the way they are used with the different meanings of fairly common words.

Preparation   Give the class some words of this kind, such as **hand**, **time**, or **cost**, to look up and elicit some of the ways they are used, pointing out that each could be used in a variety of sentences with completely different meanings. This may also be the case with the equivalent words in their own language, forming commonly used expressions which any advanced learner needs to know. Show them how the different meanings are marked in a dictionary entry, e.g. for **hand**: parts of body, help, on clock/watch, etc.

Explain that many of the lexical patterns tested in Gapped sentences involve collocations. Tell them to read grammar page R48 in the *Oxford Advanced Learner's Dictionary* and then go on to other entries, making sure that they can spot the collocations (separation by a slash, the use of bold type for important ones).

1   Study the example (0) in the exam task. Ask which words they think collocate with the missing word in the first sentence (high), the second (serious) and third (make a). They will probably suggest a number of possibilities, but stress that there are no marks for thinking of a word that fits just one sentence, or even two. Explain that 'sound' or 'part', for instance, are possible with 'high'; 'matter', 'subject' or 'topic' with 'serious'; 'record' or 'list' with 'make (a)' — but not with any of the others. If there is time, go through the dictionary entries for words they suggest, checking the different meanings to see if they fit the collocation and the context. Then ask them to look up the noun **note**. The following collocations are given: 'high/low notes' (in music), 'on a more serious note' (quality) and 'make a note' (to remind you).

2   They do questions 1–4, which all require the completion of collocations in the three sentences. For each item, tell them to check each word they think of with their dictionary, until they come up with one that fits all three sentences.

3   They check their answers with the explanatory key when they have finished.

4   Point out that collocations are tested in other task types, such as multiple-choice cloze.

Key word transformations

- CAE Use of English, Part 5
- FCE Use of English, Part 4

Key word transformations test the ability to form structures and lexical phrases with a precise overall meaning. As the focus here is not on individual words but on the phrase or sentence level, candidates need to be able to recognize and use a wide variety of forms, including verb patterns.

Preparation   Tell the class to read grammar pages R36–39 of the *Oxford Advanced Learner's Dictionary* and check that they understand what the various codes (e.g. VNN: transitive verb with two objects) stand for. You may want to work through some more verbs from the dictionary, such as **tell**, that have a number of meanings and associated patterns. In each case, remind the class that entries for verbs often show these patterns in more than one way: the code, the pattern in bold type, and the example(s).

1   Check the class know what they have to do in the exam task opposite, in particular the number of words they can use, (this will be different in other Cambridge exams).

2   Ask about the example, in particular what the key word is (**likened**). Get them to look up the entry for it in their dictionary: it gives the pattern 'liken sth/sb to sth/sb' and an example sentence using 'likened to'. The meaning given is 'compare one thing or person to another and say they are similar'. Point out that this is the sense of the first sentence, reminding the class that where verbs have several possible patterns, it will be necessary to choose the correct meaning. Emphasize the importance of maintaining the same verb tense and other information from the first sentence. To do so in this case requires using the maximum permitted number of words: 'have likened weather conditions there to'.

3   They do questions 1–4, which all require a change of verb pattern. In each case they look up the key word in their dictionary and study the patterns associated with it.

4   They check their answers with the explanatory key.

For FCE Use of English, Part 4, see the *Oxford Wordpower Dictionary*, study pages S14–15.

Worksheet 9

Gapped sentences

For questions 1–3, think of **one** word only which can be used appropriately in all three sentences. Here is an example (0).

Example:

0 Caroline is an excellent singer, but she couldn't quite reach that very high .... at the end of the song.

Friday's school party was great fun, but on a more serious .... , I'm afraid I have some sad news about one of our pupils.

It's best to make a .... of everyone's names and addresses so that you don't forget them later.

Example: *note*

1 Our aim in walking 500 miles is to .... the record for the amount of money raised for charity.

First, ... the yoghurt and curry paste together to form a thick creamy sauce.

As the enormous black and red spider moved closer, Sam's heart began to .... faster.

2 There's no need to go into any more detail: you've made your .... and we will bear in mind what you say.

Kevin had failed the exam twice and his teacher didn't see the .... of him taking it again.

After a week lost in the desert, they reached the .... where they had no water left.

3 Before she went to university, Paula had led an extremely sheltered .... and had seen very little of the world.

Convicted of the horrific crime, he was sentenced to .... imprisonment, with a recommendation to serve 35 years.

The brave firefighter risked her .... to save a child from the burning building.

Key word transformations

For questions 1–4, complete the second sentence so that it has a similar meaning to the first sentence, using the word given. **Do not change the word given.** You must use between **three** and **six** words, including the word given. Here is an example (0).

Example:

0 Scientists have said weather conditions there are like those in Antarctica.

likened

Scientists .... those in Antarctica.

Scientists *have likened weather conditions there to those in Antarctica.*

1 Last year, the school managed to reduce electricity consumption by 15%.

succeeded

The school .... electricity consumption by 15% last year.

2 For several minutes, we didn't realise what had actually happened.

took

It .... what had actually happened.

3 The lifeguard said to the three boys that they shouldn't go into the sea during the storm.

warned

The lifeguard .... into the sea during the storm.

4 By bidding for the item now, you are promising that you will buy it.

committing

By bidding for the item now, you .... it.

Using a learner's dictionary
for tests of listening

As with preparation for reading tasks, a good dictionary can help students build the vocabulary they need for successful comprehension of listening texts at all levels. It can also be used to develop a broad knowledge of synonyms and antonyms, often used in task types of all kinds where the correct answer paraphrases what is heard on the recording. Noting down the correct pronunciation of new vocabulary will also help learners understand the words when they hear them, as will listening to the recordings of words on the *Oxford Essential Dictionary CD-ROM*, the *Oxford Wordpower Dictionary CD-ROM*, and the *Oxford Advanced Learner's Compass*.

Worksheet 10
Using the Oxford Essential Dictionary

Multiple-choice questions
- FCE Listening, Part 4
- CAE Listening, Part 3
- PET Listening, Part 2

In the fourth part of FCE Listening, candidates have to listen to a single text and answer seven questions, choosing the correct answer from three alternatives in each case. Items may test gist, opinion, attitude, main idea, or specific information. Often the correct option paraphrases the information in the text.

Students therefore need to be able to recognize the same idea expressed in different ways. For suggestions on developing knowledge of synonyms and synonymous phrases, see the notes accompanying Reading Worksheets 1 (True/False) and 2 (Multiple matching) on pages 4 and 6 of this booklet.

Preparation Explain to the class that Listening items often use synonyms, or parallel expressions, to paraphrase what they hear, so they should listen out for words or phrases with similar meaning to the key words in the questions.

1 They study the multiple-choice questions opposite, highlighting the key word in each stem (the question or unfinished statement) and in each of options A, B, and C.

2 They read the transcript and answer the questions, in each case highlighting the matching expressions in the text.

3 They check their answers to the multiple-choice questions and their matching expressions with the explanatory key.

This activity is also relevant to FCE Listening, Part 1.

For CAE Listening, Part 3, see the Synonyms and Which Word? boxes in the *Oxford Advanced Learner's Dictionary*.
For PET Listening Part 2, see the Which Word? boxes in the *Oxford Essential Dictionary*.

Sentence completion
- FCE Listening, Part 2
- CAE Listening, Part 2
- PET Listening, Part 3

In the third part of FCE Listening, candidates hear a single text and have to write between one and three words in gaps in written sentences. They may need to listen for details, which can include figures of various kinds. This can create difficulties, especially where numbers are spoken in different ways in their own language. For example, the year 1990 may translate as 'one thousand, nine hundred and ninety', not 'nineteen ninety'.

Preparation Begin with the Reference section of the *Oxford Wordpower Dictionary*, pages R23–26. Go through each part with the class, paying particular attention to the way the following are spoken: large numbers, phone numbers, temperatures, the main units of measurement, dates, years, ages and times. Then test them by writing new ones on the board and asking students to say them aloud, for example:

325km   33rd   11 June   55cm   10.52 a.m.
1989   34°C   62kg   17/4/07   017 348 2998.

1 Tell the class to do parts A and B of the activity opposite.

2 When they have finished, they check with the explanatory key.

3 Ask them how each of the answers is pronounced.

For PET Listening, Part 3, see the Study Pages in the *Oxford Essential Dictionary*, pages S6–9.
For CAE Listening, Part 2, see the Reference Section in the *Oxford Advanced Learner's Dictionary*, pages R63–68.

Worksheet 10

Multiple-choice questions

Read the instructions, underline the key words in the questions and then answer them using the transcript extract below. Underline the words in the transcript that tell you the answers.

> You will hear an extract from an interview with Dr Emily Jones, a scientist who is studying the effects of climate change. For questions 1 and 2, choose the best answer (**A**, **B** or **C**).

1 What does Dr Jones say might happen because of rising temperatures?
   A There could be less water in the Mediterranean Sea.
   B Water may cover some parts of Malta.
   C Malta might end up completely under water.

2 Where is most of Malta's supply of fresh water at present?
   A On top of the salt water underground.
   B In huge metal tanks built under the island.
   C On the land, close to the farms that need it.

> **Int:** So how will the changing climate affect a Mediterranean island such as Malta?
>
> **EJ:** The most obvious effects will be caused by rising sea levels, resulting from the hotter climate we'll have in the future. Low-lying areas of the island could eventually find themselves flooded, which would be disastrous for such a densely populated place.
>
> **Int:** And what other consequences could there be?
>
> **EJ:** Well, Malta is very unusual in that despite its generally dry weather, which will become hotter and drier of course, there is a huge amount of drinkable water in natural tunnels right underneath the island. In fact, because fresh water is lighter than salt water, it actually floats on the sea water down there. But as the level of the Mediterranean rises, so the salt water will mix with the fresh, making it useless for the farmers who currently depend on it for their crops.

Sentence completion

A Read the exam instructions and questions 1–3. What kind of number is needed for each answer?

B Fill in the answers by referring to the transcript extract below.

> You will hear part of an interview with someone talking about a strange event in a small village. For questions 1–3, complete the sentences.

1 She says the village is just over .... **(1)** away.

2 The village stands at a height of .... **(2)**.

3 She first went to the village in the winter of .... **(3)**.

> 'It's a tiny place of only about 100 people, a little more than 200 kilometres from here. In winter it's often cut off from the rest of the country by heavy snow, which blocks the railway lines and the roads through the mountain passes. This is not altogether surprising as it is 2500 metres above sea level, surrounded by mountains of up to 3500 metres with a permanent covering of deep snow and ice. The days there can be sunny and even warm, but as night falls so does the temperature, sometimes reaching 25 degrees below zero. I remember going there once as a child, I think it was during that really cold December of 1998, when it was 35 below. I'd never been there before and I thought it must be like that all the time in winter.'

Using a learner's dictionary
for tests of speaking

Students can use their dictionary to prepare for the Speaking papers of all three exams. They will need to demonstrate accurate use of vocabulary, in many respects as in the Writing papers.

Students should therefore make it clear in their vocabulary notebooks which words are marked in their dictionary as *formal, informal, slang*, and so on. Students should also, where possible, learn to understand and use phonetic symbols, as shown, for example, on page viii of the *Oxford Wordpower Dictionary*. They can then note down the pronunciation of any words they find difficult. They can also listen to the recordings of individual words on the *Oxford Essential Dictionary CD-ROM*, the *Oxford Wordpower Dictionary CD-ROM*, and the *Oxford Advanced Learner's Compass*.

Worksheet 11
Using the Oxford Essential Dictionary

Answering questions about yourself
- PET Speaking, Part 1
- FCE Speaking, Part 1

In Part 1 of PET Speaking, the examiner first asks each candidate a series of simple questions: their name, where they live, and what they do. Then they are asked about learning English, their daily lives and/or their future plans. They are not expected to have perfect pronunciation, but need to make themselves understood. Difficulties can arise with even basic words, often because of the confusing way English words are spelt.

Preparation   In addition to following the advice above, learners can ensure they pronounce some of these words correctly by using the Pronunciation notes next to certain entries in the *Oxford Wordpower Dictionary*. Ask the class what the word **yacht** rhymes with, or sounds like. They will probably say something like 'matched'. Tell them to look it up: as the note explains, it actually sounds like 'hot'.

Give the class more practice with this by writing the following words on the board and asking them to match each word in group A with a word in group B, without looking at their dictionaries. Then let them check their answers in the *Oxford Wordpower Dictionary* by looking up the words in A.

A aunt   bury   cause   cough   daughter   design   doubt   draw   fruit   great   height   iron   juice   low   money   phrase   shirt   thumb   tongue   warm

B days   out   very   hurt   come   loose   off   water   lion   white   storm   late   funny   young   more   boot   fine   doors   plant   go

Answers: aunt/plant, bury/very, cause/doors, cough/off, daughter/water, design/fine, doubt/out, draw/more, fruit/boot, great/late, height/white, iron/lion, juice/loose, low/go, money/funny, phrase/days, shirt/hurt, thumb/come, tongue/young, warm/storm

1   For the role-play opposite, put students into new pairs.

2   Allow time to ask each other all the questions. Monitor and give feedback, especially on pronunciation.

3   They change roles.

For FCE Speaking, see the *Oxford Wordpower Dictionary*, S38 (Learning vocabulary) and S48 (Pronunciation).

Describing a picture
- PET Speaking, Part 3

In Part 3 of PET Speaking, candidates are given a photograph and asked to talk about it on their own for about a minute. The testing focus is their vocabulary range and their ability to organize language.

It is not sufficient merely to point at objects and name them, or describe each one individually; they should say where the objects (or people) are in relation to each other. They will need to be able to use prepositions of location to do this.

Preparation   Tell the class to look at study page S2 of the *Oxford Essential Dictionary*. Check they are familiar with all the prepositions used on the page and get them to work through exercises 1 and 2. Then go through the answers with them, using the key on page 486.

1   Put them into pairs and refer them to the speaking activity on the opposite page. Explain that they are taking the roles of candidates in PET Speaking, Part 3, using pictures in the Picture Dictionary section of the *Oxford Essential Dictionary*.

2   They practise saying where objects are in relation to each other and then do the same with people. Monitor and give feedback, especially on their use of prepositions of location.

3   As a follow-up, pairs could describe what they can see in the classroom, and say where other students are in relation to each other.

Worksheet 11

Answering questions about yourself

1 Make sure you know how to pronounce these words. Check with the notes in the *Oxford Essential Dictionary*.

> answer could birth some should
> right learn know use though
> ought half buy enough friend buy

2 Sit with another student who you don't know very well. Take the roles of examiner and candidate. Ask the following questions.

  • What's your name? How do you spell your surname?

  • Where do you live? *or* Where do you come from?

  • What subjects do you study? *or* What job to do you do?

  • Do you enjoy studying English? Why?

  • Do you think that English will be useful to you in the future?

  • What did you do last weekend?

  • What do you enjoy doing in your free time?

3 Now change roles and answer the same questions.

4 Tell each other if you found any important words difficult to understand.

Describing a picture

In PET Speaking Part 3, the examiner will give you a colour photograph and ask you to talk about it for one minute. Your partner will be given a photo relating to the same topic. Practise this using the *Oxford Essential Dictionary* by following steps 1–6.

1 Form a pair with another student and decide who will speak first.

2 Look at the picture of a house on page P10 of the *Picture Dictionary*. Describe what's in the kitchen and in the bedroom. Talk for about a minute, using these words and phrases:

> above below in between among
> beside behind opposite against under
> on top of next to in front of

3 Your partner does the same, talking about the living room and the bathroom. Listen without interrupting while he or she speaks.

4 Look at the picture of a classroom on page P11 of the *Picture Dictionary*. Briefly describe the people, then say where they are in relation to each other and to the objects there.

5 Your partner looks at the picture of a basketball match on page 14 of the *Picture Dictionary* and does the same.

6 Tell your partner what he or she did well, and suggest some improvements. Then listen to what he or she says about your speaking.

Exam task types and Worksheets

This table shows the main task types in all three exams, together with the Worksheets in this booklet that focus on each one. The Worksheets in [brackets] are also relevant to these task types. In addition, preparation for all task types will benefit from the use of dictionaries to expand vocabulary.

Cambridge Preliminary English Test (PET)

Paper		Task type	Activity
Reading	Part 1:	multiple choice (notices, etc.)	Worksheet 1
	Part 2:	matching	[Worksheet 2]
	Part 3:	true/false	Worksheet 1
	Part 4:	multiple choice	
	Part 5:	multiple-choice cloze	Worksheet 7
Writing	Part 1:	sentence transformations	Worksheet 7
	Part 2:	short communicative message	Worksheet 4
	Part 3:	story	Worksheet 4
		letter	Worksheet 5
Listening	Part 1:	multiple choice (pictures)	
	Part 2:	multiple choice	Worksheet 10
	Part 3:	gap-fill	Worksheet 10
	Part 4:	true/false	[Worksheet 1]
Speaking	Part 1:	spoken questions	Worksheet 11 [1]
	Part 2:	two-way interaction	
	Part 3:	individual long turn	Worksheet 11 [1]
	Part 4:	general conversation	

Cambridge First Certificate in English (FCE) *from December 2008*

Paper		Task type	Activity
Reading	Part 1:	multiple choice	Worksheet 3
	Part 2:	gapped text (sentences)	Worksheet 2
	Part 3:	multiple matching	Worksheet 2
Writing	Part 1:	formal letter	Worksheet 6
		informal letter or email	[Worksheet 5]
	Part 2:	article	Worksheet 6 [2]
		letter	Worksheet 5, 6
		essay	Worksheet 5
		story	Worksheet 4
		report, review or set books task	
Use of English	Part 1:	multiple-choice cloze	[Worksheet 7]
	Part 2:	open cloze	Worksheet 8
	Part 3:	word formation	Worksheet 8
	Part 4:	key word transformations	Worksheet 9

Listening	Part 1:	multiple choice	[Worksheet 3, 10]
	Part 2:	sentence completion	Worksheet 10
	Part 3:	multiple matching	
	Part 4:	multiple choice	Worksheet 3, 10
Speaking	Part 1:	spoken questions	Worksheet 11 [1]
	Part 2:	individual long turn	
	Part 3:	two-way collaborative task	
	Part 4:	three-way discussion	

Cambridge Certificate in Advanced English (CAE) *from December 2008*

Paper		Task type	Activity
Reading	Part 1:	multiple choice (short texts)	Worksheet 3
	Part 2:	gapped text (paragraphs)	Worksheet 3
	Part 3:	multiple choice	Worksheet 3
	Part 4:	multiple matching	[Worksheet 2]
Writing	Part 1:	article	Worksheet 6 [2]
		formal letter	Worksheet 6 [2]
		report, proposal	
	Part 2:	article	Worksheet 2
		formal letter	Worksheet 2
		informal letter	Worksheet 5
		essay	Worksheet 5
		report, proposal, competition entry	
		review, contribution, set books task	
Use of English	Part 1:	multiple-choice cloze	[Worksheet 7]
	Part 2:	open cloze	Worksheet 8
	Part 3:	word formation	Worksheet 8
	Part 4:	gapped sentences	Worksheet 9
	Part 5:	key word transformations	Worksheet 9
Listening	Part 1:	multiple choice (short extracts)	[Worksheet 3]
	Part 2:	sentence completion	Worksheet 10
	Part 3:	multiple choice	Worksheet 10 [3]
	Part 4:	multiple matching	
Speaking	Part 1:	spoken questions	
	Part 2:	individual long turn	
	Part 3:	two-way conversation	
	Part 4:	three-way discussion	

Explanatory Key

Reading

Worksheet 1

True/False

1 **A** The adjective 'lovely' has the same meaning as 'beautiful' and the text says these beaches are 'not far' from the city. The opposite of near is 'far'.

2 **A** Climbing over the bridge costs $100, but going 'on foot' (= walking) is 'free': in other words you don't have to pay.

3 **B** The text says a 'water taxi' costs $50, but it's actually 'cheaper' (the opposite of 'expensive') to take a ferry. The ferry to Manly is then given as an example.

4 **B** The text advises taking a ferry back at 'sunset', which is the opposite of 'sunrise'. The word 'dawn' has the same meaning as 'sunrise', so this statement is incorrect.

Multiple choice (notices, messages, etc.)

1 **B** Here, the meaning of 'may not' is 'not allowed to', NOT 'is not possible to' (A), or 'does not happen' (C).

2 **A** 'Shall' is used here to suggest something, with 'instead' indicating a change of place. It is not a request for information (B), and there is no suggestion of a change of day, or cancellation (C).

3 **B** 'For sale' means the owner wants to sell, not buy (A), it. The figure of £30 could change as she says 'or best offer' (i.e. if nobody wants to pay that much). 'Hardly' means 'almost not', and therefore does not suggest 'bad condition' (C).

Worksheet 2

Gapped text (sentences)

1 **B** The word 'this' refers back to the situation described in the previous sentence; 'modem' (and 'wireless') forms a lexical set with 'connection' and 'Internet'. See the entry for **Internet** in the *Oxford Wordpower Dictionary*.

2 **C** The phrasal verb 'logged on' forms a lexical set with 'key in' and 'password'. There is also the repetition of 'secured'/'secure', and the tense sequence 'the next time you want to', 'you key in', 'when you have logged on' and 'will be unable'. See the entry for **computers**.

3 **A** There is the lexical set formed by 'receiving', 'email' and 'sender', as well as 'downloading' and 'virus'. 'These' refer back to 'files' and 'documents', and also forward to 'these' in the following sentence. See the entry for **Internet**.

Multiple matching

1 **B** The main clue is 'on your own' in the text and 'alone' in the answer. The words 'studio', 'compact, making the most of the available space' (i.e. 'tiny') also point to a place for one person.

2 **D** The word 'cleaning' in the answer is covered by 'do ... housework' in the text.

3 **C** One clue in the answer is 'area' which corresponds to 'district' in the text. The other is 'quiet': the text says 'well away from the noise of the city centre'.

4 **A** The clue 'walking and cycling' in the text is included in 'outdoor activities' in the text, with the verb 'likes' having a similar meaning to 'keen on'.

Worksheet 3

Gapped text (paragraphs)

1 **B** The first paragraph of the main text begins 'Programmes of this nature'. Here, the phrase 'of this nature' refers back to 'documentaries on the theme of the increasing number of older people in society'. In the entry for **nature** in the Oxford Advanced Learner's Dictionary, meaning 5 (type/kind) gives the example 'things of that nature'.

2 **A** This begins 'All the same', a concession link that introduces a point ('the age profile of the population is likely to change significantly') that accepts – though only to a limited extent – that the 'wholly improbable scenario' in the first paragraph has a basis in fact. This linking expression can be found in meaning 3 (idm = idiom) of the entry for **same**, which gives the meaning as 'despite this'. Also, the second paragraph begins 'Conversely', which contrasts the 'decline' in people under 15 (end of paragraph A) with the 'rise' in the number of over-65s.

3 **C** The expression 'On account of this' begins this paragraph, making a cause/effect link between the reference to the growing number of older people in paragraph 2 to a 'reduction in the working population'. The idm (idiom) section of the entry for **account** gives the form 'on account of sb/sth', with the meaning 'because of' and the example 'she retired early on **account** of ill health'.

Multiple-choice questions

1 **C** The writer stresses that the study 'is not yet complete', using 'seems to', 'apparently', and 'the researchers say' to distance herself from the study, but she says 'they may have a point' and that the findings 'will be interesting'. She is, therefore, neither 'convinced' (A) nor 'dismissive' (D), at least not yet, but does not express the kind of doubts implied by the word 'sceptical' (B).

2 **B** The tone of the second paragraph ('growing tendency', 'come to a stop every time', 'whatever the subject') and the assertion 'it's frustrating for everyone else' do not indicate indifference (A), nor – the 'weak smile' is theirs, not hers – amusement (D). Neither is there any sympathy: 'They may feel it's a sign of efficiency, but the reality is ...' (C). Her general tone is critical, and she ends by saying it's 'extremely bad manners' (B).

Writing

Worksheet 4

Story

1 **Immediately** (not impeding) **2 disappeared** (not impeding) **3 except** (possibly impeding) **4 lose** (possibly impeding) **5 opposite** (not impeding) **6 until** (not impeding) **7 piece** (possibly impeding) **8 address** (not impeding)

Message

1 **lunch (or dinner)** Chris suggests 'noon' so this is for a midday meal. The Culture note after the entry for **meal** in the *Oxford Essential Dictionary* gives the answer.

2 **bake/roast/boil/fry** The Word Building note after **cook** gives all these verbs.

3 **cod, salmon, etc.** The Word Building note after the entry for **fish** gives these.

4 **potatoes, beans, etc.** The entry for **vegetable** gives some examples, and cross-refers to page 9 of the Picture Dictionary. Many possibilities are shown there.

5 **mango, pineapple, etc.** The Word Building note after the entry for **fruit** gives examples such as apples and bananas, and the entry also cross-refers to page 8 of the Picture Dictionary.

Worksheet 5

Essay

> **introduction:** *nowadays*
> **more information:** *furthermore/moreover/firstly*
> **consequences:** *therefore*
> **giving examples:** *for instance*
> **opinions:** *in my opinion*
> **contrast:** *however/on the other hand*
> **conclusion:** *to conclude*

1 **Nowadays** This introduces the topic and sets the time context, with a verb form ('is imported') indicating the present.

2 **However** A contrast is required here and only 'however' fits.

3 **Firstly** This introduces the initial point made in favour of the statement.

4 **Furthermore/Moreover** This introduces the second point in favour.

5 **On the other hand** This paragraph deals with the opposing arguments, so a contrast link is needed. 'On the other hand' would not fit 2, so it must go here, introducing the first point against.

6 **for instance** The sentence gives 'citrus fruits' as an example of what is produced.

7 **Therefore** The 'increased energy consumption' is a consequence of the claim that 'heating would be required' in the previous sentence.

8 **Moreover/Furthermore** This introduces the second point against.

9 **To conclude** This introduces the summing-up of the two main arguments against the statement.

10 **In my opinion** The writer's own view ('it would be a mistake') is given in the final sentence.

Informal letter

1 **Dear** – to greet the reader

2 **How** – to ask about the reader

3 **sorry** – to apologize

4 **I'm writing to** – to say why you are writing

5 **hearing from you** – to ask for a reply

6 **Love/Best wishes, etc.** – to close the letter

7 **P.S.** – to add extra information at the end.

Worksheet 6

Article

Suggested answer:

It was about three years ago, I think, when I first saw people breaking a block of wood with their bare hands. My first thought was 'Ouch!' and my second was 'I'll never be able to do that'. Then I saw a tiny eleven-year-old casually walk up and do it, and I said to myself, 'Why not?'

Since then, apart from one month when I was injured, I've been to Taekwondo classes three times a week, reaching green belt. My aim is to become a black belt in three years' time. The training is hard but fun, and it makes you feel good about yourself: stronger, fitter and more confident. You make new friends, too, particularly among those you've started out with.

Formal letter

1 **Ms Henderson** not 'Dear Maria' – *Dear* + title + surname, in a formal letter

2 **post/position** not 'job' here

3 **today's** '2day's' is text message shorthand

4 **information** not 'info'

5 **advertisement** not 'ad'

6 **extremely/very** not 'dead'

7 **details** not 'stuff'

8 **a lot of/considerable** not 'loads of'

9 **people** not 'guys'

10 **I am ('I'm')** – full form required

11 **children** not 'kids'

12 **Consequently/Therefore,** etc. not 'So'

13 **great** not 'gr8' – text message shorthand again

14 **Furthermore/In addition,** etc. not 'And'

15 **believe/think** not 'reckon'

16 **in view of the fact (that)/as,** etc. not 'seeing as how'

17 **knowledgeable about** not 'clued-up on'

18 **part/region,** etc. not 'bit'

19 **father** not 'dad'

20 **friends** not 'mates'

Vocabulary and grammar

Worksheet 7

Sentence transformations

1 **too** The key word is 'enough' and the testing focus is the contrast between the negative plus 'big' and the positive plus 'small'. The Grammar note on the *Oxford Essential Dictionary* entry for **enough** explains that 'too' is used in this context.

2 **allowed to/permitted to** Here, 'let' is the key word and the structure that changes is the active form to the passive. The difficulty here, as explained in the Grammar note to the entry for **let**, is that it is not used in the passive. The alternative 'allow' is given, and that can be used here.

3 **could see** The testing focus is on changing direct to reported speech using the key word 'can'. The Grammar note on the entry for **can** explains that the past form is 'could'.

4 **their** The change of structure is from 'in each … there is' to 'all … have … own', in which 'own' is the key word. The Grammar note on the entry for **own** warns against using *a* or *the*, showing it is instead preceded by the possessive. As 'rooms' are third person plural, this must be 'their'.

5 **such a** The structure changes from *so* + adjective, to something + adjective + noun. The key word is 'so'. The Grammar note on the entry for **so** explains that before adjective + noun the correct word is 'such'. As in the example, before a countable noun the article 'a' is added.

Multiple-choice cloze

1 **B** As the Which Word? note in the *Oxford Essential Dictionary* entry for **some** explains, 'some' is used in statements whereas 'any' is correct in questions or after 'not' – neither of which is the case here. The entry for **lot** makes it clear that it must follow 'a', while the examples with **much** show it used with uncountables, not plurals like 'countries'.

2 **A** The entry for 'job' includes a cross-reference to the Which Word? note on the entry for **work**, which says it is impossible to say 'a work', but 'a job' is correct. The dictionary explains that a **task** is a particular piece of work and that **duty** can have a similar meaning: neither is possible in this context.

3 **D** The Which Word? note on the entry for **travel** states that the correct phrase is 'the journey to work' ('there' in the text). The entry for **voyage** says that this word is for travelling by sea or in space, while neither of the meanings given for **tour** fits here.

4 **C** The noun that collocates with the missing verb is 'shopping', as in the Which Word? note at **do** (*do* or *make*?). The entry for **pay** shows, through examples, that it takes 'for' with a direct object, which is not the case before 'most of the shopping'. Neither of the meanings given in the entry for **spend** ('money' or 'time') is correct here.

5 **C** There are cross-references to Which Word? at the entry for **see**, which explains the differences. The entry for **watch** has 'watched television' (the one at **see** is to a specific programme, not TV in general). As the note makes clear, **looking** would require 'at', but would still be incorrect, and the entry for **hear** explains that it is for sound only.

Worksheet 8

Open cloze

1 **on/onto** The correct particle with 'got' is being tested here. Of the many phrasal verbs in the *Oxford Wordpower Dictionary* entry for **get**, those which actually mean 'leave a bus' and 'climb on a bus' are 'get off' and 'get on/onto'. Owing to the context ('after a few miles', it cannot be 'get off'.

2 **down/up** The verb is 'slowed' for which the entry for **slow** (*verb*) gives just two phrasal verbs. The meaning 'move at a slower speed' reflects the following verb: 'stopped'.

3 **broken** Here the particle 'down' is given, with the clues 'old' and 'holding up all the traffic'. They indicate the car can't move, in other words it has 'broken down'. The entry for the phrasal verb **break down** says 'used about a vehicle', 'stop working'.

4 **off** Again the verb is 'got' and the particle is required, and this time it is the opposite of 'get on/onto' in 1: 'she walked quickly through the hall'.

5 **in** A particle with 'checked' is needed. The *Oxford Wordpower Dictionary* entry for **check** says 'to go to a desk (or 'counter') in … an airport'.

6 **take** The particle 'off' is given. Answering this requires knowing which verb is used to describe a 'plane' departing. The entry for **take off** says 'used about an aircraft', 'to leave the ground and start flying'.

Word formation

1 **fashionable** An adjective is required before the noun 'items'. The note for the suffix -**able** on reference page S22 of the *Oxford Wordpower Dictionary* says 'to make adjectives', with the meaning 'possible to'.

2 **attractive** An adjective is needed before 'manner'. Reference page S22 says -**ive** is used 'to make adjectives' and means 'having a particular quality'. It is also an example on page xvi of Wordpower Workout.

3 **appearance** A noun is needed here, following 'the'. The note for -**ance** on reference page S22 says 'to make nouns', and one of the meanings given is 'state'.

4 **assistants** The word 'shop' is used as an adjective here, so a noun is needed. Reference page S22 says -**ant** is used 'to make nouns', and is for 'a person who does sth'. The use of 'all' indicates this noun must be plural.

5 **helpful** The word needed here refers back to 'they' and therefore must be a noun, with a positive sense (like 'friendly'). The suffix -**ful** on reference page S22 is used 'to make adjectives' and means 'having a particular quality'.

6 **overcharge** The use of 'to' and the following noun show that verb is needed, in the infinitive form. Here, a prefix is needed. Reference page S22 says that **over-** means 'more than normal' or 'too much'. The latter is actually used in the next sentence of the text; see reference page S21 ('too much', as in text).

Worksheet 9

Gapped sentences

1 **beat** 'Record' collocates with 'win', 'hold', 'set', 'break', 'equal', etc., but none of these fit the other sentences. The form 'X and Y together' could go with verbs such as 'mix' and 'stir', but these don't collocate with 'record' or 'heart'. Words that go with 'heart' include 'ache', 'leap' and 'sink', but only 'beat' makes complete sense with 'faster'. The *Oxford Advanced Learner's Dictionary* entry for **beat** gives '– A and B together' (mix), 'heart is … beating' (of heart/drums/wings) and 'beat the record' (be better).

2 **point** The noun 'sense' is possible with 'didn't see', 'case' with 'you've made your' and 'situation' with 'reached'; but none of these can go with the other sentences. The dictionary entry for **point** gives 'made your point' (opinion/fact), 'don't see the point of' (purpose) and 'reached the point' (time or stage) as collocations.

3 **life** 'Existence' and 'childhood' are possible with 'sheltered', 'immediate' with 'imprisonment', and 'neck' with 'risk', but not with any of the others. The following collocations are in the entry for **life**: 'sheltered lives' (experience/ activities), 'life imprisonment' (punishment) and 'risked his life' (state of living).

Key word transformations

1 **succeeded in reducing** The first pattern using **succeed** in the *Oxford Advanced Learner's Dictionary* entry is ' – in doing sth', with the meaning 'achieve sth'. The code is v, so no object is needed. This is similar to 'managed to' in the first sentence. An example ('succeed in getting a place') is also given.

2 **took us several minutes to realise** The dictionary gives many uses of take, but the correct one here is 'time' (29), code VNN (transitive, two objects). The relevant example is 'it took her three hours to repair her bike'. The form *took several minutes for us to realise* is not possible here as that would be seven words.

3 **warned the three boys against going** The second use given in the entry for **warn** is ' – (sb) against/about sth' (VN), followed by the relevant meaning and example 'warns against walking alone'. The form 'warned the three boys not to go' is seven words long.

4 **are committing yourself to buying** The third use of **commit** in its entry ('promise/say definitely') has a similar meaning to the first sentence, and has the VN pattern ' – sb/yourself (to sth/to doing sth)'. The relevant example is 'before committing themselves to taking out a loan'.

Listening

Worksheet 10

Multiple-choice questions

1 **B** The key expression in the stem is 'because of rising temperatures', so the phrase 'resulting from the hotter climate' indicates that the answer will follow soon. She refers to 'rising sea levels', so A is incorrect. The key expression in B is 'cover some parts', which matches 'areas … flooded'. She only says this could affect 'low-lying areas', making C impossible.

2 **A** The question word is 'where' and the key expression 'fresh water'. The speaker first refers to 'drinkable water', which is the same. This is, she says, 'underneath the island' (underground) and it 'floats on the sea water' (on top of the salt water), so A is correct. The water is in 'natural tunnels', not metal tanks, so B is wrong. Although the farmers 'depend on it' (need it), the water is under the land, not on it (C).

Sentence completion

A 1 **distance** (km/miles)

2 **altitude** (metres/feet)

3 **year** (19-something or 20-something)

B 1 **200/two hundred km/kilometres** Although the first figure heard is '100', this relates to the number of inhabitants, not the distance. The clues are 'a little more than' ('just over'), and after the answer: 'from here' ('away').

2 **2500/two thousand five hundred m/metres** The figure comes before the phrase 'above sea level' (at a height of), not to be confused with '3500 metres', which is the height of the surrounding mountains.

3 **1998/nineteen ninety-eight** The numbers '25' and '35' refer to temperatures, not years. The first clue is 'I remember going there once as a child', then the reference to 'that really cold December', followed by 'I'd never been there before'. Finally, she mentions 'winter' (so it wasn't an Australian December).

Using a dictionary for exams includes 11 worksheets to use with these dictionaries:

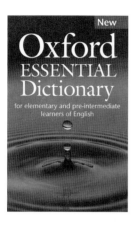

ELEMENTARY AND PRE-INTERMEDIATE
Available with CD-ROM

Helps students learn the most important words in English and how to use them. Includes 2000 keywords from the Oxford 3000™.

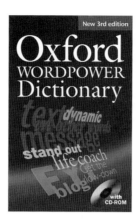

INTERMEDIATE
Available with CD-ROM

Builds students' wordpower – fast! Includes the Oxford 3000™ keywords – the most important words to learn in English.

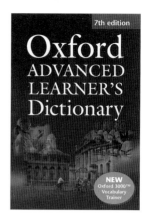

UPPER-INTERMEDIATE TO ADVANCED
Available with CD-ROM

The world's best-selling advanced learner's dictionary with more words than any other learner's dictionary at this level.

NEW Now available with *Oxford 3000™ Vocabulary Trainer.*

ALSO AVAILABLE

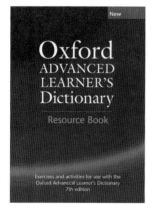

Oxford Advanced Learner's Dictionary Resource Book

64 pages, including photocopiable worksheets to help students get more from their dictionary. Includes advice on using dictionaries in class.

FREE online – *www.oup.com/elt/oald*

Access *OALD 7* online, find out more about the Oxford 3000™, download activities, and keep up to date with new words.

ALSO RECOMMENDED FOR STUDENTS WHO WANT TO ACHIEVE MORE IN ENGLISH

Oxford Student's Dictionary
Includes the words students need to study subjects such as maths, science, computing and literature – in English. *Available with CD-ROM.*

NEW 2nd edition

Oxford Collocations Dictionary
UPPER-INTERMEDIATE TO ADVANCED
Over 150,000 collocations to help students sound more natural in English.

Oxford Idioms Dictionary
INTERMEDIATE AND ABOVE
Over 10,000 idioms from British and American English explained and illustrated.

Oxford Phrasal Verbs Dictionary
INTERMEDIATE AND ABOVE
Over 7,000 phrasal verbs from British and American English.

Oxford Guide to British and American Culture
UPPER-INTERMEDIATE TO ADVANCED
An A-Z dictionary of everything you need to know about British and American culture.

Oxford Learner's Thesaurus
UPPER-INTERMEDIATE TO ADVANCED
17,000 synonyms and opposites from British and American English, with help for learners with choosing the right word for the context. *Available with CD-ROM.*